Death etc.

By the same author

Plays

Ashes to Ashes • *Betrayal* • *The Birthday Party* • *The Caretaker* • *Celebration
and The Room* • *The Collection and The Lover* • *The Hothouse* • *Landscape
and Silence* • *Moonlight* • *Mountain Language* • *No Man's Land* • *Old Times* •
One for the Road • *Other Places* • *(A Kind of Alaska, Victoria Station, Family
Voices)* • *Party Times* • *The Room and The Dumb Waiter* • *A Slight Ache
and Other Plays* • *Tea Party and Other Plays*

Plays One
*(The Birthday Party, The Room, The Dumb Waiter, A Slight Ache,
The Hothouse, A Night Out, The Black and White, The Examination)*

Plays Two
*(The Caretaker, The Dwarfs, The Collection, The Lover, Night School,
Trouble in the Works, The Black and White, Request Stop,
Last to Go, Special Offer)*

Plays Three
*(The Homecoming) Tea Party, The Basement, Landscape, Silence, Night, That's
Your Trouble, That's All, Applicant, Interview, Dialogue for Three, Old Times,
No Man's Land)*

Plays Four
*(Betrayal, Monologue, One for the Road, Family Voices, A Kind of Alaska,
Victoria Station, Mountain Language, Precisely, The New World Order,
Party Time, Moonlight, Ashes to Ashes)*

Screenplays
*The Comfort of Strangers and Other Screenplays
(Reunion, Victory, Turtle Diary)
The French Lieutenant's Woman and Other Screenplays
(The Last Tycoon, Langrishe, Go Down)
The Heal of the Day
The Proust Screenplay
The Servant and Other Screenplays (The Pumpkin Eaters,
The Quiller Memorandum, Accident, The Go-Between)
The Trial*

Poetry and Prose
*Collected Poems and Prose
The Dwarfs: A Novel*
100 *Poems by* 100 *Poets* (an anthology selected by Harold Pinter,
Geoffrey Godbert, and Anthony Astbury)
99 *Poems in Translation* (an anthology selected by Harold Pinter,
Geoffrey Godbert, and Anthony Astbury)
Various Voices: Prose, Poetry, Politics

HAROLD PINTER

Death etc.

Grove Press
New York

Printed in the United States of America

Library of Congress Cataloging-in-Publication Data

Pinter, Harold, 1930-
     Death etc. / Harold Pinter.
        p. cm.
     Includes author's "Wilfred Owen Award" speech, given on Mar. 18, 2005.
     ISBN 0-8021-4225-7
     I. Title.
   PR6066.I53D43 2005
   822'.914—dc22

                                                                              2005050203

Grove Press
841 Broadway
New York, NY 10003

05   06   07   08   09   10   9   8   7   6   5   4   3   2

To Donald and Patty, Ariel and
Angelica and Wally and Deborah

CONTENTS

CONTENTS

Death etc.

WILFRED OWEN AWARD SPEECH

This is a true honor. Wilfred Owen was a great poet. He articulated the tragedy, the horror, and indeed the pity—of war—in a way no other poet has. Yet we have learnt nothing. Nearly one hundred years after his death, the world has become more savage, more brutal, more pitiless.

But the "free world" we are told (as embodied in the United States and Great Britain) is different to the rest of the world, since our actions are dictated and sanctioned by a moral authority and a moral passion condoned by someone called God. Some people may find this difficult to comprehend, but Osama bin Laden finds it easy.

What would Wilfred Owen make of the invasion of Iraq? A bandit act, an act of blatant state terrorism, demonstrating absolute contempt for the concept of international law. An arbitrary military action inspired by a series of lies upon lies and gross manipulation of the media and therefore of the public. An act intended to consolidate American military and economic control of the Middle East masquerading—as a last resort (all other justifications having failed to justify themselves)—as liberation. A formidable assertion of military force responsible for the death and mutilation of thousands upon thousands of innocent people.

An independent and totally objective account of the Iraqi civilian dead in the medical magazine *The Lancet* estimates that the figure approaches one hundred thousand. But neither the United States nor the United Kingdom bother to count the Iraqi dead. As General Tommy Franks (U.S. Central Command) memorably said, "We don't do body counts."

We have brought torture, cluster bombs, depleted uranium, innumerable acts of random murder, misery, and degradation to the Iraqi people and call it "bringing freedom and democracy to the Middle East." But, as we all know, we have not been welcomed with the predicted flowers. What we have unleashed is a ferocious and unremitting resistance, mayhem, and chaos.

You may say at this point, What about the Iraqi elections? Well, President Bush himself answered this question only the other day when he said, "We cannot accept that there can be free democratic elections in a country under foreign military occupation."

I had to read that statement twice before I realized that he was talking about Lebanon and Syria.

What do Bush and Blair actually see when they look at themselves in the mirror?

I believe Wilfred Owen would share our contempt, our revulsion, our nausea, and our shame at both the language and the actions of the American and British governments.

March 18, 2005

DEMOCRACY

There's no escape.
The big pricks are out.
They'll fuck everything in sight.
Watch your back.

March 2003

MOUNTAIN
LANGUAGE

CHARACTERS

Mountain Language was first performed at the National Theatre in London on October 20, 1988. The cast was as follows:

YOUNG WOMAN   Miranda Richardson
ELDERLY WOMAN   Eileen Atkins
SERGEANT   Michael Gambon
OFFICER   Julian Wadham
GUARD   George Harris
PRISONER   Tony Haygarth
HOODED MAN   Alex Hardy
SECOND GUARD   Douglas McFerran

Designer   Michael Taylor
Director   Harold Pinter

I
A PRISON WALL

A line of women. An ELDERLY WOMAN, *cradling her hand.*
A basket at her feet.

A YOUNG WOMAN *with her arm around the Woman's*
shoulders.

A SERGEANT *enters, followed by an* OFFICER. *The Sergeant*
points to the Young Woman.

SERGEANT   Name?

YOUNG WOMAN   We've given our names.

SERGEANT   Name?

YOUNG WOMAN   We've given our names.

SERGEANT   Name?

OFFICER (*to Sergeant*)   Stop this shit. (*to Young Woman*) Any
    complaints?

YOUNG WOMAN   She's been bitten.

OFFICER   Who?

Pause.

OFFICER (*cont.*)   Who? Who's been bitten?

YOUNG WOMAN   She has. She has a torn hand. Look. Her
    hand has been bitten. This is blood.

SERGEANT (*to Young Woman*)   What is your name?

OFFICER Shut up.

He walks over to Elderly Woman.

OFFICER (*cont.*) What's happened to your hand? Has someone bitten your hand?

The Woman slowly lifts her hand. He peers at it.

OFFICER (*cont.*) Who did this? Who bit you?

YOUNG WOMAN A Doberman pinscher.

OFFICER Which one?

Pause.

OFFICER (*cont.*) Which one?

Pause.

OFFICER (*cont.*) Sergeant!

Sergeant steps forward.

SERGEANT Sir!

OFFICER Look at this woman's hand. I think the thumb is going to come off. (*to Elderly Woman*) Who did this?

She stares at him.

OFFICER (*cont.*) Who did this?

YOUNG WOMAN A big dog.

OFFICER What was his name?

Pause.

OFFICER (*cont.*) What was his *name*?

Pause.

OFFICER (*cont.*)   Every dog has a *name*! They answer to
their name. They are given a name by their parents and
that is their name, that is their *name*! Before they bite,
they *state* their name. It's a formal procedure. They state
their name and then they bite. What was his name? If you
tell me one of our dogs bit this woman without giving his
name I will have that dog shot!

Silence.

OFFICER (*cont.*)   Now—attention! Silence and attention!
Sergeant!

SERGEANT   Sir?

OFFICER   Take any complaints.

SERGEANT   Any complaints? Has anyone got any
complaints?

YOUNG WOMAN   We were told to be here at nine o'clock
this morning.

SERGEANT   Right. Quite right. Nine o'clock this morning.
Absolutely right. What's your complaint?

YOUNG WOMAN   We were here at nine o'clock this
morning. It's now five o'clock. We have been standing
here for eight hours. In the snow. Your men let
Doberman pinschers frighten us. One bit this woman's
hand.

OFFICER   What was the name of this dog?

She looks at him.

YOUNG WOMAN   I don't know his name.

SERGEANT   With permission sir?

OFFICER   Go ahead.

SERGEANT   Your husbands, your sons, your fathers, these men you have been waiting to see, are shithouses. They are enemies of the State. They are shithouses.

The Officer steps toward the Women.

OFFICER   Now hear this. You are mountain people. You hear me? Your language is dead. It is forbidden. It is not permitted to speak your mountain language in this place. You cannot speak your language to your men. It is not permitted. Do you understand? You may not speak it. It is outlawed. You may only speak the language of the capital. That is the only language permitted in this place. You will be badly punished if you attempt to speak your mountain language in this place. This is a military decree. It is the law. Your language is forbidden. It is dead. No one is allowed to speak your language. Your language no longer exists. Any questions?

YOUNG WOMAN   I do not speak the mountain language.

Silence. The Officer and Sergeant slowly circle her. The Sergeant puts his hand on her bottom.

SERGEANT   What language do you speak? What language do you speak with your arse?

OFFICER   These women, Sergeant, have as yet committed no crime. Remember that.

SERGEANT   Sir! But you're not saying they're without sin?

OFFICER   Oh, no. Oh, no, I'm not saying that.

SERGEANT   This one's full of it. She bounces with it.

OFFICER   She doesn't speak the mountain language.

The Woman moves away from the Sergeant's hand and turns to face the two men.

YOUNG WOMAN   My name is Sara Johnson. I have come to see my husband. It is my right. Where is he?

OFFICER   Show me your papers.

She gives him a piece of paper. He examines it, turns to Sergeant.

OFFICER (*cont.*)   He doesn't come from the mountains. He's in the wrong batch.

SERGEANT   So is she. She looks like a fucking intellectual to me.

OFFICER   But you said her arse wobbled.

SERGEANT   Intellectual arses wobble the best.

Blackout.

VISITORS ROOM

A PRISONER *sitting. The Elderly Woman sitting, with basket. A* GUARD *standing behind her.*

The Prisoner and the Woman speak in a strong rural accent.

Silence.

ELDERLY WOMAN   I have bread—

The Guard jabs her with a stick.

GUARD   Forbidden. Language forbidden.

She looks at him. He jabs her.

GUARD (*cont.*)   It's forbidden. (*to Prisoner*) Tell her to speak the language of the capital.

PRISONER   She can't speak it.

Silence.

PRISONER (*cont.*)   She doesn't speak it.

Silence.

ELDERLY WOMAN   I have apples—

The Guard jabs her and shouts.

GUARD   Forbidden! Forbidden forbidden forbidden! Jesus Christ! (*to Prisoner*) Does she understand what I'm saying?

PRISONER   No.

GUARD Doesn't she?

He bends over her.

GUARD (*cont.*) Don't you?

She stares up at him.

PRISONER She's old. She doesn't understand.

GUARD Whose fault is that?

He laughs.

GUARD (*cont.*) Not mine, I can tell you. And I'll tell you another thing. I've got a wife and three kids. And you're all a pile of shit.

Silence.

PRISONER I've got a wife and three kids.

GUARD You've what?

Silence.

GUARD (*cont.*) You've got what?

Silence.

GUARD (*cont.*) What did you say to me? You've got what?

Silence.

GUARD (*cont.*) You've got *what*?

He picks up the telephone and dials one digit.

GUARD (*cont.*) Sergeant? I'm in the Blue Room . . . yes . . . I thought I should report, Sergeant . . . I think I've got a joker in here.

Lights to half. The figures are still.

Voices over:

ELDERLY WOMAN'S VOICE   The baby is waiting for you.

PRISONER'S VOICE   Your hand has been bitten.

ELDERLY WOMAN'S VOICE   They are all waiting for you.

PRISONER'S VOICE   They have bitten my mother's hand.

ELDERLY WOMAN'S VOICE   When you come home there will be such a welcome for you. Everyone is waiting for you. They're all waiting for you. They're all waiting to see you.

Lights up. The Sergeant comes in.

SERGEANT   What joker?

Blackout.

3
VOICE IN THE DARKNESS

SERGEANT'S VOICE   Who's that fucking woman? What's that fucking woman doing here? Who let that fucking woman through that fucking door?

SECOND GUARD'S VOICE   She's his wife.

Lights up.

A corridor.

A HOODED MAN *held up by the Guard and the Sergeant. The Young Woman at a distance from them, staring at them.*

SERGEANT   What is this, a reception for Lady Duck Muck? Where's the bloody Babycham? Who's got the bloody Babycham for Lady Duck Muck?

He goes to the Young Woman.

SERGEANT (*cont.*)   Hello, miss. Sorry. A bit of a breakdown in administration, I'm afraid. They've sent you through the wrong door. Unbelievable. Someone'll be done for this. Anyway, in the meantime, what can I do for you, dear lady, as they used to say in the movies?

Lights to half. The figures are still.

Voices over:

MAN'S VOICE   I watch you sleep. And then your eyes open. You look up at me above you and smile.

YOUNG WOMAN'S VOICE   You smile. When my eyes open
I see you above me and smile.

MAN'S VOICE   We are out on a lake.

YOUNG WOMAN'S VOICE   It is spring.

MAN'S VOICE   I hold you. I warm you.

YOUNG WOMAN'S VOICE   When my eyes open I see you
above me and smile.

*Lights up. The Hooded Man collapses. The Young Woman
screams.*

YOUNG WOMAN   Charley!

The Sergeant clicks his fingers. The Guard drags the Man off.

SERGEANT   Yes, you've come in the wrong door. It must
be the computer. The computer's got a double hernia.
But I'll tell you what—if you want any information on
any aspect of life in this place, we've got a bloke comes
into the office every Tuesday week, except when it rains.
He's right on top of his chosen subject. Give him a tinkle
one of these days and he'll see you all right. His name is
Dokes. Joseph Dokes.

YOUNG WOMAN   Can I fuck him? If I fuck him, will
everything be all right?

SERGEANT   Sure. No problem.

YOUNG WOMAN   Thank you.

Blackout.

4
VISITORS ROOM

Guard. Elderly Woman. Prisoner.

Silence.

The Prisoner has blood on his face. He sits trembling. The Woman is still. The Guard is looking out of a window. He turns to look at them both.

GUARD Oh, I forgot to tell you. They've changed the rules. She can speak. She can speak in her own language. Until further notice.

PRISONER She can speak?

GUARD Yes. Until further notice. New rules.

Pause.

PRISONER Mother, you can speak.

Pause.

PRISONER *(cont.)* Mother, I'm speaking to you. You see? We can speak. You can speak to me in our own language.

She is still.

PRISONER *(cont.)* You can speak.

Pause.

PRISONER *(cont.)* Mother. Can you hear me? I am speaking to you in our own language.

Pause.

PRISONER (*cont.*)   Do you hear me?

Pause.

PRISONER (*cont.*)   It's our language.

Pause.

PRISONER (*cont.*)   Can't you hear me? Do you hear me?

She does not respond.

PRISONER (*cont.*)   Mother?

GUARD   Tell her she can speak in her own language. New rules. Until further notice.

PRISONER   Mother?

She does not respond. She sits still.

The Prisoner's trembling grows. He falls from the chair onto his knees, begins to gasp and shake violently.

The Sergeant walks into the room and studies the Prisoner shaking on the floor.

SERGEANT (*to Guard*)   Look at this. You go out of your way to give them a helping hand and they fuck it up.

Blackout.

THE DISAPPEARED

Lovers of light, the skulls,
The burnt skin, the white
Flash of the night,
The heat in the death of men.

The hamstring and the heart
Torn apart in a musical room,
Where children of the light
Know that their kingdom has come.

1998

THE NEW
WORLD ORDER

The New World Order was first performed on July 19, 1991, at the Royal Court Theatre Upstairs, London. The cast was as follows:

DES   Bill Paterson
LIONEL   Michael Byrne
BLINDFOLDED MAN   Douglas McFerran

Director   Harold Pinter
Designer   Ian MacNeil
Lighting   Kevin Sleep

A blindfolded man sitting on a chair. Two men (DES and LIONEL) looking at him.

DES Do you want to know something about this man?

LIONEL What?

DES He hasn't got any idea at all of what we're going to do to him.

LIONEL He hasn't, no.

DES He hasn't, no. He hasn't got any idea at all about any one of the number of things that we might do to him.

LIONEL That we will do to him.

DES That we will.

Pause.

DES (*cont.*) Well, some of them. We'll do some of them.

LIONEL Sometimes we do all of them.

DES That can be counterproductive.

LIONEL Bollocks.

They study the man. He is still.

DES But anyway here he is, here he is sitting here, and he hasn't the faintest idea of what we might do to him.

LIONEL Well, he probably has the *faintest* idea.

DES A faint idea, yes. Possibly.

Des bends over the man.

DES (*cont.*) Have you? What do you say?

He straightens.

DES (*cont.*)   Let's put it this way. He has *little* idea of what we might do to him, of what in fact we are about to do to him.

LIONEL   Or his wife. Don't forget his wife. He has little idea of what we're about to do to his wife.

DES   Well, he probably has *some* idea, he's probably got *some* idea. After all, he's read the papers.

LIONEL   What papers?

Pause.

DES   You're right there.

LIONEL   Who is this cunt anyway? What is he, some kind of peasant—or a lecturer in theology?

DES   He's a lecturer in fucking peasant theology.

LIONEL   Is he? What about his wife?

DES   Women don't have theological inclinations.

LIONEL   Oh, I don't know. I used to discuss that question with my mother—quite often.

DES   What question?

LIONEL   Oh you know, the theological aspirations of the female.

Pause.

DES   What did she say?

LIONEL   She said . . .

DES What?

Pause.

LIONEL I can't remember.

He turns to the man in the chair.

LIONEL (*cont.*) Motherfucker.

DES Fuckpig.

They walk around the chair.

LIONEL You know what I find really disappointing?

DES What?

LIONEL The level of ignorance that surrounds us. I mean, this prick here—

DES You called him a cunt last time.

LIONEL What?

DES You called him a cunt last time. Now you call him a prick. How many times do I have to tell you? You've got to learn to define your terms and stick to them. You can't call him a cunt in one breath and a prick in the next. The terms are mutually contradictory. You'd lose face in any linguistic discussion group, take my tip.

LIONEL Christ. Would I?

DES Definitely. And you know what it means to you. You know what language means to you.

LIONEL Yes, I do know.

DES Yes, you do know. Look at this man here, for example. He's a first-class example. See what I mean? Before he came in here he was a big shot, he never stopped shooting his mouth off, he never stopped questioning received ideas. Now—because he's apprehensive about what's about to happen to him—he's stopped all that, he's got nothing more to say, he's more or less called it a day. I mean once—not too long ago—this man was a man of conviction, wasn't he, a man of principle. Now he's just a prick.

LIONEL Or a cunt.

DES And we haven't even finished with him. We haven't begun.

LIONEL No, we haven't even finished with him. We haven't even finished with him! Well, we haven't begun.

DES And there's still his wife to come.

LIONEL That's right. We haven't finished with him. We haven't even begun. And we haven't finished with his wife either.

DES We haven't even begun.

Lionel puts his hand over his face and sobs.

DES (*cont.*) What are you crying about?

LIONEL I love it. I love it. I love it.

He grasps Des's shoulder.

LIONEL (*cont.*) Look. I have to tell you. I've got to tell you. There's no one else I can tell.

DES   All right. Fine. Go on. What is it? Tell me.

Pause.

LIONEL   I feel so pure.

Pause.

DES   Well, you're right. You're right to feel pure. You know why?

LIONEL   Why?

DES   Because you're keeping the world clean for democracy.

They look into each other's eyes.

DES *(cont.)*   I'm going to shake you by the hand.

Des shakes Lionel's hand. He then gestures to the man in the chair with his thumb.

DES *(cont.)*   And so will he . . . *(he looks at his watch)* . . . in about thirty-five minutes.

Blackout.

ONE FOR THE ROAD

One for the Road was first performed at the Lyric Theatre Studio, Hammersmith, on March 13, 1984. The cast was as follows:

NICOLAS *Mid 40s*   Alan Bates
VICTOR *30*   Roger Lloyd Pack
GILA *30*   Jenny Quayle
NICKY *7*   Stephen Kember or Felix Yates

Director   Harold Pinter

The BBC-TV production, transmitted on July 25, 1985, had the same cast except that Rosie Kerslake played Gila and Paul Adams played Nicky. It was directed by Kenneth Ives.

One for the Road was subsequently presented as part of the triple bill *Other Places* at the Duchess Theatre, London, from March 7 to June 22, 1985, with the following cast:

NICOLAS   Colin Blakely
VICTOR   Roger Davidson
GILA   Rosie Kerslake
NICKY   Daniel Kipling or Simon Vyvyan

Director   Kenneth Ives

One for the Road was also performed at the New Ambassadors, London, July 2000, and at Lincoln Center, New York, July 2001. The cast was as follows:

NICOLAS   Harold Pinter
VICTOR   Lloyd Hutchinson
GILA   Indira Varma
NICKY   Rory Copus

Director   Robin Lefevre

A ROOM. MORNING.

NICOLAS *at his desk. He leans forward and speaks into a machine.*

NICOLAS   Bring him in.

He sits back. The door opens. VICTOR *walks in, slowly. His clothes are torn. He is bruised. The door closes behind him.*

NICOLAS *(cont.)*   Hello! Good morning. How are you? Let's not beat about the bush. Anything but that. *D'accord?* You're a civilized man. So am I. Sit down.

Victor slowly sits.

Nicolas stands, walks over to him.

NICOLAS *(cont.)*   What do you think this is? It's my finger. And this is my little finger. I wave my big finger in front of your eyes. Like this. And now I do the same with my little finger. I can also use both . . . at the same time. Like this. I can do absolutely anything I like. Do you think I'm mad? My mother did.

He laughs.

NICOLAS *(cont.)*   Do you think waving fingers in front of people's eyes is silly? I can see your point. You're a man of the highest intelligence. But would you take the same view if it was my boot—or my penis? Why am I so obsessed with eyes? Am I obsessed with eyes? Possibly. Not my eyes. Other people's eyes. The eyes of people who are brought to me here. They're so vulnerable. The soul shines through them. Are you a religious man? I am. Which side do you think God is on? I'm going to have a drink.

He goes to sideboard, pours whiskey.

NICOLAS (*cont.*) You're probably wondering where your wife is. She's in another room.

He drinks.

NICOLAS (*cont.*) Good-looking woman.

He drinks.

NICOLAS (*cont.*) God, that was good.

He pours another.

NICOLAS (*cont.*) Don't worry, I can hold my booze.

He drinks.

NICOLAS (*cont.*) You may have noticed I'm the chatty type. You probably think I'm part of a predictable, formal, long-established pattern; i.e., I chat away, friendly, insouciant, I open the batting, as it were, in a lighthearted, even carefree manner, while another waits in the wings, silent, introspective, coiled like a puma. No, no. It's not quite like that. I run the place. God speaks through me. I'm referring to the Old Testament God, by the way, although I'm a long way from being Jewish. Everyone respects me here. Including you, I take it? I think that is the correct stance.

Pause.

NICOLAS (*cont.*) Stand up.

Victor stands.

NICOLAS (*cont.*) Sit down.

Victor sits.

NICOLAS (*cont.*)   Thank you so much.

Pause.

NICOLAS (*cont.*)   Tell me something. . . .

Silence.

NICOLAS (*cont.*)   What a good-looking woman your wife is. You're a very lucky man. Tell me . . . one for the road, I think. . . .

He pours whiskey.

NICOLAS (*cont.*)   You do respect me, I take it?

He stands in front of Victor and looks down at him. Victor looks up.

NICOLAS (*cont.*)   I would be right in assuming that?

Silence.

VICTOR (*quietly*)   I don't know you.

NICOLAS   But you respect me.

VICTOR   I don't know you.

NICOLAS   Are you saying you don't respect me?

Pause.

NICOLAS (*cont.*)   Are you saying you would respect me if you knew me better? Would you like to know me better?

Pause.

NICOLAS (*cont.*)   Would you like to know me better?

VICTOR What I would like . . . has no bearing on the matter.

NICOLAS Oh yes it has.

Pause.

NICOLAS (*cont.*) I've heard so much about you. I'm terribly pleased to meet you. Well, I'm not sure that *pleased* is the right word. One has to be so scrupulous about language. Intrigued. I'm intrigued. Firstly because I've heard so much about you. Secondly because if you don't respect me you're unique. Everyone else knows the voice of God speaks through me. You're not a religious man, I take it?

Pause.

NICOLAS (*cont.*) You don't believe in a guiding light?

Pause.

NICOLAS (*cont.*) What then?

Pause.

NICOLAS (*cont.*) So . . . morally . . . you flounder in wet shit. You know . . . like when you've eaten a rancid omelet.

Pause.

NICOLAS (*cont.*) I think I deserve one for the road.

He pours, drinks.

NICOLAS (*cont.*) Do you drink whiskey?

Pause.

NICOLAS (*cont.*) I hear you have a lovely house. Lots of books. Someone told me some of my boys kicked it around a bit. Pissed on the rugs, that sort of thing. I wish they wouldn't do that. I do really. But you know what it's like—they have such responsibilities—and they feel them—they are constantly present, day and night, these responsibilities—and so, sometimes, they piss on a few rugs. You understand. You're not a fool.

Pause.

NICOLAS (*cont.*) Is your son all right?

VICTOR I don't know.

NICOLAS Oh, I'm sure he's all right. What age is he . . . seven . . . or thereabouts? Big lad, I'm told. Nevertheless, silly of him to behave as he did. But is he all right?

VICTOR I don't know.

NICOLAS Oh, I'm sure he's all right. Anyway, I'll have a word with him later and find out. He's somewhere on the second floor, I believe.

Pause.

NICOLAS (*cont.*) Well now . . .

Pause.

NICOLAS (*cont.*) What do you say? Are we friends?

Pause.

NICOLAS (*cont.*) I'm prepared to be frank, as a true friend should. I love death. What about you?

41

Pause.

NICOLAS (*cont.*)   What about you? Do you love death? Not necessarily your own. Others. The death of others. Do you love the death of others, or at any rate, do you love the death of others as much as I do?

Pause.

NICOLAS (*cont.*)   Are you always so dull? I understood you enjoyed the cut and thrust of debate.

Pause.

NICOLAS (*cont.*)   Death. Death. Death. Death. As has been noted by the most respected authorities, it is beautiful. The purest, most harmonious thing there is. Sexual intercourse is nothing compared to it.

He drinks.

NICOLAS (*cont.*)   Talking about sexual intercourse . . .

He laughs wildly, stops.

NICOLAS (*cont.*)   Does she . . . fuck? Or does she . . . ? Or does she . . . like . . . you know . . . what? What does she like? I'm talking about your wife. Your *wife*.

Pause.

NICOLAS (*cont.*)   You know the old joke? Does she fuck?

Heavily, in another voice:

NICOLAS (*cont.*)   Does she fuck!

He laughs.

NICOLAS (*cont.*)   It's ambiguous, of course. It could mean she fucks like a rabbit or she fucks not at all.

Pause.

NICOLAS (*cont.*)   Well, we're all God's creatures. Even your wife.

Pause.

NICOLAS (*cont.*)   There is only one obligation. *To be honest.* You have no other obligation. Weigh that. In your mind. Do you know the man who runs this country? No? Well, he's a very nice chap. He took me aside the other day— last Wednesday, I think it was—he took me aside at a reception, visiting dignitaries, he took *me* aside, *me,* and he said to me, he said, in what I can only describe as a hoarse whisper, Nic, he said, Nic (that's my name), Nic, if you ever come across anyone whom you have good reason to believe is getting on my tits, tell them one thing, tell them honesty is the best policy. The cheese was superb. Goat. One for the road.

He pours.

NICOLAS (*cont.*)   Your wife and I had a very nice chat, but I couldn't help noticing she didn't look her best. She's probably menstruating. Women do that.

Pause.

NICOLAS (*cont.*)   You know, old chap, I do love other things, apart from death. So many things. Nature. Trees, things like that. A nice blue sky. Blossoms.

Pause.

NICOLAS (*cont.*)   Tell me . . . truly . . . are you beginning to love me?

Pause.

NICOLAS (*cont.*)   I think your wife is. Beginning. She is beginning to fall in love with me. On the brink . . . of doing so. The trouble is, I have rivals. Because everyone here has fallen in love with your wife. It's her eyes have beguiled them. What's her name? Gila . . . or something?

Pause.

NICOLAS (*cont.*)   Who would you prefer to be? You or me?

Pause.

NICOLAS (*cont.*)   I'd go for me if I were you. The trouble about you, although I grant your merits, is that you're on a losing wicket, while I can't put a foot wrong. Do you take my point? Ah, God, let me confess, let me make a confession to you. I have never been more moved, in the whole of my life, as when—only the other day, last Friday, I believe—the man who runs this country announced to the country: We are all patriots, we are as one, we all share a common heritage. Except you, apparently.

Pause.

NICOLAS (*cont.*)   I feel a link, you see, a bond. I share a commonwealth of interest. I am not alone. I am not alone!

Silence.

VICTOR   Kill me.

NICOLAS What?

VICTOR Kill me.

Nicolas goes to him, puts his arm around him.

NICOLAS What's the matter?

Pause.

NICOLAS (*cont.*) What in heaven's name is the matter?

Pause.

NICOLAS (*cont.*) Mmmnnn?

Pause.

NICOLAS (*cont.*) You're probably just hungry. Or thirsty. Let me tell you something. I hate despair. I find it intolerable. The stink of it gets up my nose. It's a blemish. Despair, old fruit, is a cancer. It should be castrated. Indeed I've often found that that works. Chop the balls off and despair goes out the window. You're left with a happy man. Or a happy woman. Look at me.

Victor does so.

NICOLAS (*cont.*) Your soul shines out of your eyes.

Blackout.

LIGHTS UP. AFTERNOON.

Nicolas standing with a small boy.

NICOLAS What is your name?

NICKY Nicky.

NICOLAS Really? How odd.

Pause.

NICOLAS (*cont.*) Do you like cowboys and Indians?

NICKY Yes. A bit.

NICOLAS What do you really like?

NICKY I like airplanes.

NICOLAS Real ones or toy ones?

NICKY I like both kinds of ones.

NICOLAS Do you?

Pause.

NICOLAS (*cont.*) Why do you like airplanes?

Pause.

NICKY Well . . . because they go so fast. Through the air.
    The real ones do.

NICOLAS And the toy ones?

NICKY I pretend they go as fast as the real ones do.

Pause.

NICOLAS Do you like your mummy and daddy?

Pause.

NICOLAS (*cont.*) Do you like your mummy and daddy?

NICKY Yes.

NICOLAS Why?

Pause.

NICOLAS (*cont.*) Why?

Pause.

NICOLAS (*cont.*) Do you find that a hard question to answer?

Pause.

NICKY Where's Mummy?

NICOLAS You don't like your mummy and daddy?

NICKY Yes. I do.

NICOLAS Why?

Pause.

NICOLAS (*cont.*) Would you like to be a soldier when you grow up?

NICKY I don't mind.

NICOLAS You don't? Good. You like soldiers. Good. But you spat at my soldiers and you kicked them. You attacked them.

NICKY Were they your soldiers?

NICOLAS They are your country's soldiers.

NICKY I didn't like those soldiers.

NICOLAS They don't like you either, my darling.

Blackout.

ONE FOR THE ROAD

LIGHTS UP. NIGHT.

Nicolas sitting. GILA *standing. Her clothes are torn. She is bruised.*

NICOLAS   When did you meet your husband?

GILA   When I was eighteen.

NICOLAS   Why?

GILA   Why?

NICOLAS   Why?

GILA   I just met him.

NICOLAS   Why?

GILA   I didn't plan it.

NICOLAS   Why not?

GILA   I didn't know him.

NICOLAS   Why not?

Pause.

NICOLAS (*cont.*)   Why not?

GILA   I didn't know him.

NICOLAS   Why not?

GILA   I met him.

NICOLAS   When?

GILA   When I was eighteen.

NICOLAS   Why?

48

GILA   He was in the room.

NICOLAS   Room?

Pause.

NICOLAS (*cont.*)   Room?

GILA   The same room.

NICOLAS   As what?

GILA   As I was.

NICOLAS   As I was?

GILA (*screaming*)   As I was!

Pause.

NICOLAS   Room? What room?

GILA   A room.

NICOLAS   What room?

GILA   My father's room.

NICOLAS   Your father? What's your father got to do with it?

Pause.

NICOLAS (*cont.*)   Your *father*? How dare you? Fuckpig.

Pause.

NICOLAS (*cont.*)   Your father was a wonderful man. His country is proud of him. He's dead. He was a man of honor. He's dead. Are you prepared to insult the memory of your father?

Pause.

NICOLAS (*cont.*)   Are you prepared to defame, to debase, the memory of your father? Your father fought for his country. I knew him. I revered him. Everyone did. He believed in God. He didn't *think,* like you shitbags. He *lived.* He lived. He was iron and gold. He would die, he would die, he would die, for his country, for his God. And he did die, he died, he died, for his God. You turd. To spawn such a daughter. What a fate. Oh, poor, perturbed spirit, to be haunted forever by such scum and spittle. How do you dare speak of your father to me? I loved him, as if he were my own father.

Silence.

NICOLAS (*cont.*)   Where did you meet your husband?

GILA   In a street.

NICOLAS   What were you doing there?

GILA   Walking.

NICOLAS   What was he doing?

GILA   Walking.

Pause.

GILA (*cont.*)   I dropped something. He picked it up.

NICOLAS   What did you drop?

GILA   The evening paper.

NICOLAS   You were drunk.

Pause.

NICOLAS (*cont.*)   You were drugged.

Pause.

NICOLAS (*cont.*)   You had absconded from your hospital.

GILA   I was not in a hospital.

NICOLAS   Where are you now?

Pause.

NICOLAS (*cont.*)   Where are you now? Do you think you are in a hospital?

Pause.

NICOLAS (*cont.*)   Do you think we have nuns upstairs?

Pause.

NICOLAS (*cont.*)   What do we have upstairs?

GILA   No nuns.

NICOLAS   What do we have?

GILA   Men.

NICOLAS   Have they been raping you?

She stares at him.

NICOLAS (*cont.*)   How many times?

Pause.

NICOLAS (*cont.*)   How many times have you been raped?

Pause.

NICOLAS (*cont.*)   How many times?

He stands, goes to her, lifts his finger.

NICOLAS (*cont.*)   This is my big finger. And this is my little finger. Look. I wave them in front of your eyes. Like this. How many times have you been raped?

GILA   I don't know.

NICOLAS   And you consider yourself a reliable witness?

He goes to sideboard, pours drink, sits, drinks.

NICOLAS (*cont.*)   You're a lovely woman. Well, you were.

He leans back, drinks, sighs.

NICOLAS (*cont.*)   Your son is . . . seven. He's a little prick. You made him so. You have taught him to be so. You had a choice. You could have encouraged him to be a good person. Instead, you encouraged him to be a little prick. You encouraged him to spit, to strike at soldiers of honor, soldiers of God.

Pause.

NICOLAS (*cont.*)   Oh well . . . in one way I suppose it's academic.

Pause.

NICOLAS (*cont.*)   You're of no interest to me. I might even let you out of here, in due course. But I should think you might entertain us all a little more before you go.

Blackout.

ONE FOR THE ROAD

LIGHTS UP. NIGHT.

Nicolas standing.

Victor sitting. Victor is tidily dressed.

NICOLAS   How have you been? Surviving?

VICTOR   Yes.

NICOLAS   Yes?

VICTOR   Yes. Yes.

NICOLAS   Really? How?

VICTOR   Oh . . .

Pause.

NICOLAS   I can't hear you.

VICTOR   It's my mouth.

NICOLAS   Mouth?

VICTOR   Tongue.

NICOLAS   What's the matter with it?

Pause.

NICOLAS (*cont.*)   What about a drink? One for the road.
  What do you say to a drink?

He goes to the bottle, pours two glasses, gives a glass to Victor.

NICOLAS (*cont.*)   Drink up. It'll put lead in your pencil. And
  then we'll find someone to take it out.

He laughs.

NICOLAS (*cont.*)   We can do that, you know. We have a first-class brothel upstairs, on the sixth floor, chandeliers, the lot. They'll suck you in and blow you out in little bubbles. All volunteers. Their daddies are in our business. Which is, I remind you, to keep the world clean for God. Get me? Drink up. Drink up. Are you refusing to drink with me?

Victor drinks. His head falls back.

NICOLAS (*cont.*)   Cheers.

Nicolas drinks.

NICOLAS (*cont.*)   You can go.

Pause.

NICOLAS (*cont.*)   You can leave. We'll meet again, I hope. I trust we will always remain friends. Go out. Enjoy life. Be good. Love your wife. She'll be joining you in about a week, by the way. If she feels up to it. Yes. I feel we've both benefited from our discussions.

Victor mutters.

NICOLAS (*cont.*)   What?

Victor mutters.

NICOLAS (*cont.*)   What?

VICTOR   My son.

NICOLAS   Your son? Oh, don't worry about him. He was a little prick.

Victor straightens and stares at Nicolas.

Silence.

Blackout.

THE OLD DAYS

Well, there was no problem.
All the democracies
(all the democracies)

were behind us.

So we had to kill some people.
So what?
Lefties get killed.

This is what we used to say
back in the old days:

Your daughter is a lefty.

I'll ram this stinking battering ram
all the way up and up and up and up
right the way through all the way up
all the way through her lousy lefty body.

So that stopped the lefties.

THE OLD DAYS

They may have been the old days
but I'll tell you they were the good old days.

Anyway all the democracies
(all the democracies)
were behind us.

They said: just don't
(just don't)
tell anyone we're behind you.

That's all.
Just don't tell anyone
(just don't)
just don't tell anyone
we're behind you.

Just kill them.

Well, my wife wanted peace.
And so did my little children.
So we killed all the lefties
to bring peace for our little children.

Anyway there was no problem.
Anyway they're all dead anyway.

1996

PRESS CONFERENCE

Press Conference was first presented as part of an evening of sketches on February 8 and 11, 2002, at the Royal National Theatre, London. The cast was as follows:

MINISTER   Harold Pinter
PRESS   Members of the company

The company included Linda Bassett, Danny Dyer, Douglas Hodge, Patrick Marber, Kika Markham, Catherine McCormack, Corin Redgrave, Samantha Robson, Gary Shelford, Andy de la Tour, Frances de la Tour, Penelope Wilton, Susan Wooldridge, Henry Woolf

Director   Gari Jones

PRESS   Sir, before you became Minister of Culture I believe you were the head of the Secret Police.

MINISTER   That is correct.

PRESS   Do you find any contradiction between those two roles?

MINISTER   None whatsoever. As head of Secret Police it was my responsibility, specifically, to protect and to safeguard our cultural inheritance against forces which were intent upon subverting it. We were defending ourselves against the worm. And we still are.

PRESS   The worm?

MINISTER   The worm.

PRESS   As head of the Secret Police what was your policy towards children?

MINISTER   We saw children as a threat if—that is—they were the children of subversive families.

PRESS   So how did you employ your policy towards them?

MINISTER   We abducted them and brought them up properly or we killed them.

PRESS   How did you kill them? What was the method adopted?

MINISTER   We broke their necks.

PRESS   And women?

MINISTER   We raped them. It was all part of an educational process, you see. A cultural process.

PRESS What was the nature of the culture you were proposing?

MINISTER A culture based on respect and the rule of law.

PRESS How do you understand your present role as Minister of Culture?

MINISTER The Ministry of Culture holds to the same principles as the guardians of National Security. We believe in a healthy, muscular, and tender understanding of our cultural heritage and our cultural obligations. These obligations naturally include loyalty to the free market.

PRESS How about cultural diversity?

MINISTER We subscribe to cultural diversity; we have faith in a flexible and vigorous exchange of views; we believe in fecundity.

PRESS And critical dissent?

MINISTER Critical dissent is acceptable—if it is left at home. My advice is—leave it at home. Keep it under the bed. With the piss pot.

He laughs.

MINISTER (*cont.*) Where it belongs.

PRESS Did you say *in* the piss pot?

MINISTER I'll put your head in the piss pot if you're not careful.

He laughs. They laugh.

MINISTER (*cont.*) Let me make myself quite clear. We need critical dissent because it keeps us on our toes. But we don't want to see it in the marketplace or on the avenues and piazzas of our great cities. We don't want to see it manifested in the houses of any of our great institutions. We are happy for it to remain at home, which means we can pop in at any time and read what is kept under the bed, discuss it with the writer, pat him on the head, shake him by his hand, give him perhaps a minor kick up the arse or in the balls, and set fire to the whole shebang. By this method we keep our society free from infection. There is of course, however, always room for confession, retraction, and redemption.

PRESS So you see your role as Minister of Culture as vital and fruitful?

MINISTER Immensely fruitful. We believe in the innate goodness of your ordinary Jack and your ordinary Jill. This is what we seek to protect. We seek to protect the essential goodness of your ordinary Jack and your ordinary Jill. We understand that as a moral obligation. We are determined to protect them from corruption and subversion with all the means at our disposal.

PRESS Minister, thank you for your frank words.

MINISTER It has been my pleasure. Can I say one thing more?

PRESS (*various*) Please. Yes. Yes please. Please do. Yes!

MINISTER Under our philosophy . . . he that is lost is found. Thank you!

Applause. The Minister waves and exits.

Blackout.

AN OPEN LETTER TO THE
PRIME MINISTER

Dear Prime Minister,

We have been reminded often over the last few weeks of Saddam Hussein's appalling record in the field of human rights. It is indeed appalling: brutal, pathological. But I thought you might be interested to scrutinize the record of your ally, the United States, in a somewhat wider context. I am not at all certain that your advisors will have kept you fully informed.

The United States has supported, subsidized, and, in a number of cases, engendered every right-wing military dictatorship in the world since 1945. I refer to Guatemala, Indonesia, Chile, Greece, Uruguay, the Philippines, Brazil, Paraguay, Haiti, Turkey, and El Salvador, for example. Hundreds of thousands of people have been murdered by these regimes, but the money, the resources, the equipment (all kinds), the advice, the moral support, as it were, has come from successive U.S. administrations.

The deaths really do mount up: 170,000 in Guatemala, 200,000 in East Timor, 80,000 in El Salvador, 30,000 in Nicaragua, 500,000 in Indonesia—and that's just to be going on with. They are, every single one of them, attributable to your ally's foreign policy.

The devastation the United States inflicted upon Vietnam, Laos, and Cambodia, the use of napalm and Agent Orange, and the employment of new bombs which sprayed darts inside people's bodies and finally wrenched their guts out was a remorseless, savage, systematic course of destruction, which, however, failed to destroy the spirit of the Vietnamese people. When the United States was defeated, it at once set out to starve the country by way of trade embargo.

The United States invaded the Dominican Republic in 1965, Grenada in 1983, Panama in 1990, and destabilized and brought down the democratically elected governments of Guatemala, Chile, Greece, and Haiti—all acts entirely outside the parameters of international law.

It has given and still gives total support to the Turkish government's campaign of genocide against the Kurdish people. It describes the Kurdish resistance forces in Turkey as "terrorists" whereas it referred to its own vicious Contra force in Nicaragua as "freedom fighters." Its "covert" action against Nicaragua was declared by the International Court of Justice in The Hague to be in clear breach of international law.

Over the last five years the UN has passed five resolutions with overwhelming majorities demanding that the United States stop its embargo on Cuba. The United States has ignored all of them. All UN resolutions criticizing Israel have been ignored, not only by Israel but also by the United States, which turns a blind eye to Israel's nuclear capability and shrugs off Israel's oppression of the Palestinian people.

The United States possesses of course quite a handy nuclear capability itself. I would say it outstrips Saddam's ability to kill "every man, woman, and child on earth" by quite a few miles.

If that wasn't enough, it also has substantial chemical arsenals and has recently rejected two UN inspectors, one Cuban and one Iranian. It also reserves the right to deny access to certain "national security" zones. They are closed to inspection as "inspection may pose a threat to the national security interests of the United States."

Isn't Saddam Hussein saying something like that?

George Kennan, head of the U.S. State Department, setting out the ground rules for U.S. foreign policy in a "top secret" internal document in 1948, said, "We will have to dispense with all sentimentality and daydreaming and our attention will have to be concentrated everywhere on our immediate national objectives. We should cease to talk about vague and unreal objectives such as human rights, the raising of living standards, and democratization. The day is not far off when we are going to have to deal in straight power concepts. The less we are hampered by idealistic slogans the better." Kennan was an unusual man. He told the truth.

I'm sure you would agree that historical perspective is of the first importance and that a proper detachment is a crucial obligation which devolves upon leaders of men.

Anyway, this is your ally, with whom you are locked in a moral embrace.

Oh, by the way, meant to mention, forgot to tell you, we were all chuffed to our bollocks when Labour won the election.

Guardian, February 17, 1998

HOUSE OF COMMONS SPEECH

There's an old story about Oliver Cromwell. After he had taken the town of Drogheda, the citizens were brought to the main square. Cromwell announced to his lieutenants, "Right! Kill all the women and rape all the men." One of his aides said, "Excuse me, General. Isn't it the other way around?" A voice from the crowd called out, "Mr. Cromwell knows what he's doing!" That voice is the voice of Tony Blair. "Mr. Bush knows what he's doing!"

But the fact is that Mr. Bush and his gang do know what they're doing and Blair, unless he really is the deluded idiot he often appears to be, also knows what they're doing. They are determined, quite simply, to control the world and the world's resources. And they don't give a damn how many people they murder on the way. And Blair goes along with it.

He hasn't the support of the Labour Party, he hasn't the support of the country or of the celebrated "international community." How can he justify taking this country into a war nobody wants? He can't. He can only resort to rhetoric, cliché, and propaganda. Little did we think when we voted Blair into power that we would come to despise him. The idea that he has influence over Bush is laughable. His supine acceptance of American bullying is pathetic.

Bullying is of course a time-honored American tradition. In 1965, Lyndon Johnson said to the Greek Ambassador to the United States, "Fuck your parliament and your constitution. America is an elephant. Cyprus is a flea. Greece is a flea. If these two fellows continue itching the elephant they may just get whacked by the elephant's trunk, whacked good."

He meant what he said. Shortly afterward the Colonels, supported by the United States, took over, and the Greek people spent seven years in hell.

As for the American elephant, it has grown to be a monster of grotesque and obscene proportions.

The "special relationship" between the United States and the United Kingdom has, in the last twelve years, brought about the deaths of thousands upon thousands of people in Iraq, Afghanistan, and Serbia. All this in pursuit of the American and British "moral crusade" to bring "peace and stability to the world."

The use of depleted uranium in the Gulf War has been particularly effective. Radiation levels in Iraq are appallingly high. Babies are born with no brain, no eyes, no genitals. Where they do have ears, mouths, or rectums, all that issues from these orifices is blood.

Blair and Bush are of course totally indifferent to such facts, not forgetting the charming, grinning, beguiling Bill Clinton, who was apparently given a standing ovation at the Labour Party Conference. For what, killing Iraqi children? Or Serbian children?

Bush has said, "We will not allow the world's worst weapons to remain in the hands of the world's worst leaders." Quite right. Look in the mirror, chum. That's you.

The United States is at this moment developing advanced systems of "weapons of mass destruction" and is prepared to use them where it sees fit. It has walked away from international agreements on biological and chemical weapons, refusing to allow any inspection of its own factories.

It is holding hundreds of Afghans prisoner in Guantanamo Bay, allowing them no legal redress although they are charged with nothing, holding them captive virtually forever.

It is insisting on immunity from the international criminal court, a stance which beggars belief but which is now supported by Great Britain.

The hypocrisy is breathtaking.

Tony Blair's contemptible subservience to this criminal American regime demeans and dishonors this country.

October 15, 2002

GOD BLESS AMERICA

Here they go again,
The Yanks in their armored parade
Chanting their ballads of joy
As they gallop across the big world
Praising America's God.

The gutters are clogged with the dead:
The ones who couldn't join in,
The others refusing to sing,
The ones who are losing their voice,
The ones who've forgotten the tune.

The riders have whips which cut.
Your head rolls onto the sand,
Your head is a pool in the dirt,
Your head is a stain in the dust,
Your eyes have gone out and your nose
Sniffs only the pong of the dead,
And all the dead air is alive
With the smell of America's God.

January 2003

AMERICAN FOOTBALL
A reflection on the Gulf War

Hallelujah!
It works.
We blew the shit out of them.

We blew the shit right back up their own ass
And out their fucking ears.

It works.
We blew the shit out of them.
They suffocated in their own shit!

Hallelujah.
Praise the Lord for all good things.

We blew them into fucking shit.
They are eating it.

Praise the Lord for all good things.

We blew their balls into shards of dust,
Into shards of fucking dust.

We did it.

Now I want you to come over here and kiss me
on the mouth.

August 1991

IRAQ DEBATE, IMPERIAL WAR MUSEUM

Freedom, democracy, and liberation. These terms, as enunciated by Bush and Blair, essentially mean death, destruction, and chaos.

Tony Blair describes the insurgents as terrorists. There is clearly a body of foreign nationals which has entered Iraq since the invasion and which is committing terrorist atrocities. But the heart of the insurgency is widespread Iraqi resistance to a brutal and savage military occupation. Cutting off somebody's head is a barbaric act. But so is the dropping of cluster bombs on totally innocent people and tearing them apart.

Thousands upon thousands of civilians have been killed in Iraq and many thousands more mutilated for life. We don't see the corpses or the mutilated children on television.

The U.S. invasion of Iraq was not only totally unjustified, illegal, and illegitimate, it was a criminal act of immense proportions and one which will have profound consequences throughout the world.

But the invasion was also quite consistent with declared American foreign policy. American foreign policy now aims at FULL-SPECTRUM DOMINANCE—that is the U.S. administration's term, not mine. Full-spectrum dominance means control of air, sea, land, and space. It also of course means control of the world's resources.

The United States has over 700 military installations in 132 countries, including this one. It already has a vast military base at Baghdad airport. These bases are not there by accident or for "humanitarian reasons." They are there to keep a stranglehold on the world, and they will do it by any means at their disposal.

The disclosures of torture in Iraq should come as no surprise to anybody. The Americans have been exporting torture for years. They have been teaching torture techniques to military representatives of various dictatorships at Fort Benning in Georgia for a very long time. Fort Benning was called the School of Americas but was actually known as the "school of torture." They practice it themselves at home, in the vast gulag of prisons across the United States, where over two million people are held in custody, the majority black. Restraint chairs, where convicts are strapped and left naked in their own urine and excrement for days, the use of gas and stun guns, the random brutality, the systematic rape and abuse of young men and women—all of these things and more an affront to human dignity—are common practice. So torture in Iraq, at Bagram in Afghanistan, and at Guantanamo Bay are simply par for the course. That is the nature of the beast.

But the United States is not finding things so easy, and the less easy they find things the more dangerous they become. There is a growing resistance worldwide to this arrogant, brutal, complacent, destructive force, a force which holds the concept of international law and the United Nations in contempt and whose only vocabulary is bombs and death.

The United States possesses more "weapons of mass destruction" than the rest of the world put together. It is at this moment developing new nuclear systems which it is prepared to use at the drop of a hat. It is totally indifferent to the death of others and will murder anyone who gets in its way. It is the most feared, most powerful, and most detested nation the world has ever known.

The invasion of Iraq was an act of state terrorism. So it is Bush and Blair who are in fact the terrorists. I believe they must be arraigned at the International Criminal Court of Justice and tried as war criminals.

September 23, 2004

THE "SPECIAL RELATIONSHIP"

The bombs go off
The legs go off
The heads go off

The arms go off
The feet go off
The light goes out

The heads go off
The legs go off
The lust is up

The dead are dirt
The lights go out
The dead are dust

A man bows down before another man
And sucks his lust

August 2004

THE BOMBS

There are no more words to be said
All we have left are the bombs
Which burst out of our head
All that is left are the bombs
Which suck out the last of our blood
All we have left are the bombs
Which polish the skulls of the dead

February 2003

ASHES TO ASHES

Ashes to Ashes was first presented by the Royal Court Theatre at the Ambassadors Theatre, London, on September 12, 1996. The cast was as follows:

DEVLIN   Stephen Rea
REBECCA   Lindsay Duncan

Director   Harold Pinter
Designer   Eileen Diss
Lighting   Mick Hughes
Costume   Tom Rand
Sound   Torn Lishman

Time: Now

A house in the country.

Ground-floor room. A large window. Garden beyond.

Two armchairs. Two lamps.

Early evening. Summer.

The room darkens during the course of the play. The lamplight intensifies.

By the end of the play the room and the garden beyond are only dimly defined.

The lamplight has become very bright but does not illumine the room.

DEVLIN *standing with drink.* REBECCA *sitting. Both in their forties.*

Silence.

REBECCA   Well . . . for example . . . he would stand over me and clench his fist. And then he'd put his other hand on my neck and grip it and bring my head towards him. His fist . . . grazed my mouth. And he'd say, "Kiss my fist."

DEVLIN   And did you?

REBECCA   Oh yes. I kissed his fist. The knuckles. And then he'd open his hand and give me the palm of his hand . . . to kiss . . . which I kissed.

Pause.

REBECCA (*cont.*)   And then I would speak.

DEVLIN   What did you say? You said what? What did you say?

Pause.

REBECCA   I said, "Put your hand round my throat." I murmured it through his hand, as I was kissing it, but he heard my voice, he heard it through his hand, he felt my voice in his hand, he heard it there.

Silence.

DEVLIN   And did he? Did he put his hand round your throat?

REBECCA   Oh yes. He did. He did. And he held it there, very gently, very gently, so gently. He adored me, you see.

DEVLIN   He adored you?

Pause.

DEVLIN (*cont.*)   What do you mean, he adored you? What do you mean?

Pause.

DEVLIN (*cont.*)   Are you saying he put no pressure on your throat? Is that what you're saying?

REBECCA   No.

DEVLIN   What then? What are you saying?

REBECCA   He put a little ... pressure ... on my throat, yes. So that my head started to go back, gently but truly.

DEVLIN   And your body? Where did your body go?

REBECCA   My body went back, slowly but truly.

DEVLIN   So your legs were opening?

REBECCA   Yes.

Pause.

DEVLIN   Your legs were opening?

REBECCA   Yes.

Silence.

DEVLIN   Do you feel you're being hypnotized?

REBECCA   When?

DEVLIN   Now.

REBECCA   No.

DEVLIN   Really?

REBECCA   No.

DEVLIN   Why not?

REBECCA   Who by?

DEVLIN   By me.

REBECCA   You?

DEVLIN   What do you think?

REBECCA   I think you're a fuckpig.

DEVLIN   Me a fuckpig? Me! You must be joking.

Rebecca smiles.

REBECCA Me joking? You must be joking.

Pause.

DEVLIN You understand why I'm asking you these questions. Don't you? Put yourself in my place. I'm compelled to ask you questions. There are so many things I don't know. I know nothing . . . about any of this. Nothing. I'm in the dark. I need light. Or do you think my questions are illegitimate?

Pause.

REBECCA What questions?

Pause.

DEVLIN Look. It would mean a great deal to me if you could define him more clearly.

REBECCA Define him? What do you mean, define him?

DEVLIN Physically. I mean, what did he actually look like? If you see what I mean? Length, breadth . . . that sort of thing. Height, width. I mean, quite apart from his . . . disposition, whatever that may have been . . . or his character . . . or his spiritual . . . standing . . . I just want, well, I need . . . to have a clearer idea of him . . . well, not a clearer idea . . . just an idea, in fact . . . because I have absolutely no idea . . . as things stand . . . of what he looked like.

I mean, what did he *look like*? Can't you give him a shape for me, a concrete shape? I want a concrete image of him, you see . . . an image I can carry about with me. I mean, all you can talk of are his hands, one hand over your face, the other on the back of your neck, then the first one on your throat. There must be more to him than hands. What about eyes? Did he have any eyes?

REBECCA   What color?

Pause.

DEVLIN   That's precisely the question I'm asking you . . . my darling.

REBECCA   How odd to be called darling. No one has ever called me darling. Apart from my lover.

DEVLIN   I don't believe it.

REBECCA   You don't believe what?

DEVLIN   I don't believe he ever called you darling.

Pause.

DEVLIN (*cont.*)   Do you think my use of the word is illegitimate?

REBECCA   What word?

DEVLIN   Darling.

REBECCA   Oh yes, you called me darling. How funny.

DEVLIN   Funny? Why?

REBECCA   Well, how can you possibly call me darling? I'm not your darling.

DEVLIN   Yes you are.

REBECCA   Well, I don't want to be your darling. It's the last thing I want to be, I'm nobody's darling.

DEVLIN That's a song.

REBECCA What?

DEVLIN "I'm nobody's baby now."

REBECCA It's "*You're* nobody's baby now." But anyway, I didn't use the word *baby*.

Pause.

REBECCA (*cont.*) I can't tell you what he looked like.

DEVLIN Have you forgotten?

REBECCA No. I haven't forgotten. But that's not the point. Anyway, he went away years ago.

DEVLIN Went away? Where did he go?

REBECCA His job took him away. He had a job.

DEVLIN What was it?

REBECCA What?

DEVLIN What kind of job was it? What job?

REBECCA I think it had something to do with a travel agency. I think he was some kind of courier. No, No, he wasn't. That was only a part-time job. I mean that was only part of the job in the agency. He was quite high up, you see. He had a lot of responsibilities.

Pause.

DEVLIN What sort of agency?

REBECCA A travel agency.

DEVLIN   What sort of travel agency?

REBECCA   He was a guide, you see. A guide.

DEVLIN   A tourist guide?

Pause.

REBECCA   Did I ever tell you about that place . . . about the time he took me to that place?

DEVLIN   What place?

REBECCA   I'm sure I told you.

DEVLIN   No. You never told me.

REBECCA   How funny. I could swear I had. Told you.

DEVLIN   You haven't told me anything. You've never spoken about him before. You haven't told me anything.

Pause.

DEVLIN (*cont.*)   What place?

REBECCA   Oh, it was a kind of factory, I suppose.

DEVLIN   What do you mean, a kind of factory? Was it a factory or wasn't it? And if it was a factory, what kind of factory was it?

REBECCA   Well, they were making things—just like any other factory. But it wasn't the usual kind of factory.

DEVLIN   Why not?

REBECCA   They were all wearing caps . . . the workpeople . . . soft caps . . . and they took them off when he came in, leading me, when he led me down the alleys between the rows of workpeople.

DEVLIN They took their caps off? You mean they doffed them?

REBECCA Yes.

DEVLIN Why did they do that?

REBECCA He told me afterwards it was because they had such great respect for him.

DEVLIN Why?

REBECCA Because he ran a really tight ship, he said. They had total faith in him. They respected his . . . purity, his . . . conviction. They would follow him over a cliff and into the sea, if he asked them, he said. And sing in a chorus, as long as he led them. They were in fact very musical, he said.

DEVLIN What did they make of you?

REBECCA Me? Oh, they were sweet. I smiled at them. And immediately every single one of them smiled back.

Pause.

REBECCA (*cont.*) The only thing was—the place was so damp. It was exceedingly damp.

DEVLIN And they weren't dressed for the weather?

REBECCA No.

Pause.

DEVLIN I thought you said he worked for a travel agency?

REBECCA   And there was one other thing. I wanted to go to the bathroom. But I simply couldn't find it. I looked everywhere. I'm sure they had one. But I never found out where it was.

Pause.

REBECCA (*cont.*)   He did work for a travel agency. He was a guide. He used to go to the local railway station and walk down the platform and tear all the babies from the arms of their screaming mothers.

Pause.

DEVLIN   Did he?

Silence.

REBECCA   By the way, I'm terribly upset.

DEVLIN   Are you? Why?

REBECCA   Well, it's about that police siren we heard a couple of minutes ago.

DEVLIN   What police siren?

REBECCA   Didn't you hear it? You must have heard it. Just a couple of minutes ago.

DEVLIN   What about it?

REBECCA   Well, I'm just terribly upset.

Pause.

REBECCA (*cont.*)   I'm just incredibly upset.

Pause.

REBECCA (*cont.*)   Don't you want to know why? Well, I'm going to tell you anyway. If I can't tell you who can I tell? Well, I'll tell you anyway. It just hit me so hard. You see . . . as the siren faded away in my ears I knew it was becoming louder and louder for somebody else.

DEVLIN   You mean that it's always being heard by somebody, somewhere? Is that what you're saying?

REBECCA   Yes. Always. Forever.

DEVLIN   Does that make you feel secure?

REBECCA   No! It makes me feel insecure! Terribly insecure.

DEVLIN   Why?

REBECCA   I hate it fading away. I hate it echoing away. I hate it leaving me. I hate losing it. I hate somebody else possessing it. I want it to be mine, all the time. It's such a beautiful sound. Don't you think?

DEVLIN   Don't worry, there'll always be another one. There's one on its way to you now. Believe me. You'll hear it again soon. Any minute.

REBECCA   Will I?

DEVLIN   Sure. They're very busy people, the police. There's so much for them to do. They've got so much to take care of, to keep their eye on. They keep getting signals, mostly in code. There isn't one minute of the day when they're not charging around one corner or another in the world, in their police cars, ringing their sirens. So you can take comfort from that, at least. Can't you? You'll never be lonely again. You'll never be without a police siren. I promise you.

Pause.

DEVLIN (*cont.*)   Listen. This chap you were just talking about
. . . I mean this chap you and I have been talking about . . .
in a manner of speaking . . . when exactly did you meet
him? I mean when did all this happen exactly? I haven't . . .
how can I put this . . . quite got it into focus. Was it before
you knew me or after you knew me? That's a question of
some importance. I'm sure you'll appreciate that.

REBECCA   By the way, there's something I've been dying to
tell you.

DEVLIN   What?

REBECCA   It was when I was writing a note, a few notes
for the laundry. Well . . . to put it bluntly . . . a laundry
list. Well, I put my pen on that little coffee table and it
rolled off.

DEVLIN   No?

REBECCA   It rolled right off, onto the carpet. In front of my
eyes.

DEVLIN   Good God.

REBECCA   This pen, this perfectly innocent pen.

DEVLIN   You can't know it was innocent.

REBECCA   Why not?

DEVLIN   Because you don't know where it had been. You
don't know how many other hands have held it, how
many other hands have written with it, what other people
have been doing with it. You know nothing of its history.
You know nothing of its parents' history.

REBECCA A pen has no parents.

Pause.

DEVLIN You can't sit there and say things like that.

REBECCA I can sit here.

DEVLIN You can't sit there and say things like that.

REBECCA You don't believe I'm entitled to sit here? You don't think I'm entitled to sit in this chair, in the place where I live?

DEVLIN I'm saying that you're not entitled to sit in that chair or in or on any other chair and say things like that and it doesn't matter whether you live here or not.

REBECCA I'm not entitled to say things like what?

DEVLIN That that pen was innocent.

REBECCA You think it was guilty?

Silence.

DEVLIN I'm letting you off the hook. Have you noticed? I'm letting you slip. Or perhaps it's me who's slipping. It's dangerous. Do you notice? I'm in a quicksand.

REBECCA Like God.

DEVLIN God? God? You think God is sinking into a quicksand? That's what I would call a truly disgusting perception. If it can be dignified by the word perception. Be careful how you talk about God. He's the only God we have. If you let him go he won't come back. He won't even look back over his shoulder. And then what will you do? You know what it'll be like, such a vacuum? It'll be

like England playing Brazil at Wembley and not a soul in
the stadium. Can you imagine? Playing both halves to a
totally empty house. The game of the century. Absolute
silence. Not a soul watching. Absolute silence. Apart from
the referee's whistle and a fair bit of fucking and blinding. If
you turn away from God it means that the great and noble
game of soccer will fall into permanent oblivion. No score
for extra time after extra time after extra time, no score for
time everlasting, for time without end. Absence. Stalemate.
Paralysis. A world without a winner.

Pause.

DEVLIN (*cont.*) I hope you get the picture.

Pause.

DEVLIN (*cont.*) Now let me say this. A little while ago you
    made . . . shall we say . . . you made a somewhat oblique
    reference to your bloke . . . your lover? . . . and babies
    and mothers, etc. And platforms. I inferred from this that
    you were talking about some kind of atrocity. Now let
    me ask you this. What authority do you think you
    yourself possess which would give you the right to discuss
    such an atrocity?

REBECCA I have no such authority. Nothing has ever
    happened to me. Nothing has ever happened to any of
    my friends. I have never suffered. Nor have my friends.

DEVLIN Good.

Pause.

DEVLIN (*cont.*) Shall we talk more intimately? Let's talk
    about more intimate things, let's talk about something

more personal, about something within your own immediate experience. I mean, for example, when the hairdresser takes your head in his hands and starts to wash your hair very gently and to massage your scalp, when he does that, when your eyes are closed and he does that, he has your entire trust, doesn't he? It's not just your head which is in his hands, is it, it's your life, it's your spiritual . . . welfare.

Pause.

DEVLIN (*cont.*)   So you see what I wanted to know was this . . . when your lover had his hand on your throat, did he remind you of your hairdresser?

Pause.

DEVLIN (*cont.*)   I'm talking about your lover. The man who tried to murder you.

REBECCA   Murder me?

DEVLIN   Do you to death.

REBECCA   No, no. He didn't try to murder me. He didn't want to murder me.

DEVLIN   He suffocated you and strangled you. As near as makes no difference. According to your account. Didn't he?

REBECCA   No, no. He felt compassion for me. He adored me.

Pause.

DEVLIN   Did he have a name, this chap? Was he a foreigner? And where was I at the time? What do you

want me to understand? Were you unfaithful to me?
Why didn't you confide in me? Why didn't you confess?
You would have felt so much better. Honestly. You
could have treated me like a priest. You could have put
me on my mettle. I've always wanted to be put on my
mettle. It used to be one of my lifetime ambitions. Now
I've missed my big chance. Unless all this happened
before I met you. In which case you have no obligation
to tell me anything. Your past is not my business. I
wouldn't dream of telling you about my past. Not that I
had one. When you lead a life of scholarship you can't
be bothered with the humorous realities, you know, tits,
that kind of thing. Your mind is on other things, have
you got an attentive landlady, can she come up with
bacon and eggs after eleven o'clock at night, is the bed
warm, does the sun rise in the right direction, is the
soup cold? Only once in a blue moon do you wobble
the chambermaid's bottom, on the assumption there is
one—chambermaid, not bottom—but of course none of
this applies when you have a wife. When you have a
wife you let thought, ideas and reflection, take their
course. Which means you never let the best man win.
Fuck the best man, that's always been my motto. It's the
man who ducks his head and moves on through no
matter what wind or weather who gets there in the end.
A man with guts and application.

Pause.

DEVLIN (*cont.*)   A man who doesn't give a shit.
A man with a rigid sense of duty.

Pause.

DEVLIN (*cont.*)   There's no contradiction between those last
two statements. Believe me.

Pause.

DEVLIN (*cont.*)   Do you follow the drift of my argument?

REBECCA   Oh yes, there's something I've forgotten to tell
you. It was funny. I looked out of the garden window,
out of the window into the garden, in the middle of
summer, in that house in Dorset, do you remember? Oh
no, you weren't there. I don't think anyone else was
there. No. I was all by myself. I was alone. I was looking
out of the window and I saw a whole crowd of people
walking through the woods, on their way to the sea, in
the direction of the sea. They seemed to be very cold,
they were wearing coats, although it was such a beautiful
day. A beautiful, warm, Dorset day. They were carrying
bags. There were . . . guides . . . ushering them, guiding
them along. They walked through the woods and I could
see them in the distance walking across the cliff and down
to the sea. Then I lost sight of them. I was really quite
curious so I went upstairs to the highest window in the
house and I looked way over the top of the treetops and I
could see down to the beach. The guides . . . were
ushering all these people across the beach. It was such a
lovely day. It was so still and the sun was shining. And I
saw all these people walk into the sea. The tide covered
them slowly. Their bags bobbed about in the waves.

DEVLIN   When was that? When did you live in Dorset? I've
never lived in Dorset.

Pause.

REBECCA Oh, by the way, somebody told me the other day that there's a condition known as mental elephantiasis.

DEVLIN What do you mean, "somebody told" you? What do you mean, "the other day"? What are you talking about?

REBECCA This mental elephantiasis means that when you spill an ounce of gravy, for example, it immediately expands and becomes a vast sea of gravy. It becomes a sea of gravy which surrounds you on all sides and you suffocate in a voluminous sea of gravy. It's terrible. But it's all your own fault. You brought it upon yourself. You are not the *victim* of it, you are the *cause* of it. Because it was you who spilt the gravy in the first place, it was you who handed over the bundle.

Pause.

DEVLIN The what?

REBECCA The bundle.

Pause.

DEVLIN So what's the question? Are you prepared to drown in your own gravy? Or are you prepared to die for your country? Look. What do you say, sweetheart? Why don't we go out and drive into town and take in a movie?

REBECCA That's funny, somewhere in a dream . . . a long time ago . . . I heard someone calling me sweetheart.

Pause.

REBECCA (*cont.*) I looked up. I'd been dreaming. I don't know whether I looked up in the dream or as I opened my eyes. But in this dream a voice was calling. That I'm certain of. This voice was calling me. It was calling me sweetheart.

Pause.

REBECCA (*cont.*) Yes.

Pause.

REBECCA (*cont.*) I walked out into the frozen city. Even the mud was frozen. And the snow was a funny color. It wasn't white. Well, it was white but there were other colors in it. It was as if there were veins running through it. And it wasn't smooth, as snow is, as snow should be. It was bumpy. And when I got to the railway station I saw the train. Other people were there.

Pause.

REBECCA (*cont.*) And my best friend, the man I had given my heart to, the man I knew was the man for me the moment we met, my dear, my most precious companion, I watched him walk down the platform and tear all the babies from the arms of their screaming mothers.

Silence.

DEVLIN Did you see Kim and the kids?

She looks at him.

DEVLIN (*cont.*) You were going to see Kim and the kids today.

She stares at him.

DEVLIN (*cont.*) Your sister Kim and the kids.

REBECCA   Oh, Kim! And the kids, yes. Yes. Yes, of course I saw them. I had tea with them. Didn't I tell you?

DEVLIN   No.

REBECCA   Of course I saw them.

Pause.

DEVLIN   How were they?

REBECCA   Ben's talking.

DEVLIN   Really? What's he saying?

REBECCA   Oh, things like "My name is Ben." Things like that. And "Mummy's name is Mummy." Things like that.

DEVLIN   What about Betsy?

REBECCA   She's crawling.

DEVLIN   No, really?

REBECCA   I think she'll be walking before we know where we are. Honestly.

DEVLIN   Probably talking too. Saying things like "My name is Betsy."

REBECCA   Yes, of course I saw them. I had tea with them. But oh . . . my poor sister . . . she doesn't know what to do.

DEVLIN   What do you mean?

REBECCA   Well, he wants to come back . . . you know . . . he keeps phoning and asking her to take him back. He says he can't bear it, he says he's given the other one up, he says he's living quite alone, he's given the other one up.

DEVLIN Has he?

REBECCA He says he has. He says he misses the kids.

Pause.

DEVLIN Does he miss his wife?

REBECCA He says he's given the other one up. He says it was never serious, you know, it was only sex.

DEVLIN Ah.

Pause.

DEVLIN (*cont.*) And Kim?

Pause.

DEVLIN (*cont.*) And Kim?

REBECCA She'll never have him back. Never. She says she'll never share a bed with him again. Never. Ever.

DEVLIN Why not?

REBECCA Never ever.

DEVLIN But why not?

REBECCA Of course I saw Kim and the kids. I had tea with them. Why did you ask? Did you think I didn't see them?

DEVLIN No. I didn't know. It's just that you said you were going to have tea with them.

REBECCA Well, I did have tea with them! Why shouldn't I? She's my sister.

Pause.

REBECCA (*cont.*) Guess where I went after tea? To the cinema. I saw a film.

DEVLIN Oh? What?

REBECCA A comedy.

DEVLIN Uh-huh? Was it funny? Did you laugh?

REBECCA Other people laughed. Other members of the audience. It was funny.

DEVLIN But you didn't laugh?

REBECCA Other people did. It was a comedy. There was a girl . . . you know . . . and a man. They were having lunch in a smart New York restaurant. He made her smile.

DEVLIN How?

REBECCA Well . . . he told her jokes.

DEVLIN Oh, I see.

REBECCA And then in the next scene he took her on an expedition to the desert, in a caravan. She'd never lived in a desert before, you see. She had to learn how to do it.

Pause.

DEVLIN Sounds very funny.

REBECCA But there was a man sitting in front of me, to my right. He was absolutely still throughout the whole film. He never moved, he was rigid, like a body with rigor mortis, he never laughed once, he just sat like a corpse. I moved far away from him, I moved as far away from him as I possibly could.

Silence.

DEVLIN   Now look, let's start again. We live here. You don't live . . . in Dorset . . . or *anywhere else.* You live here with me. This is our house. You have a very nice sister. She lives close to you. She has two lovely kids. You're their aunt. You like that.

Pause.

DEVLIN *(cont.)*   You have a wonderful garden. You love your garden. You created it all by yourself. You have truly green fingers. You also have beautiful fingers.

Pause.

DEVLIN *(cont.)*   Did you hear what I said? I've just paid you a compliment. In fact I've just paid you a number of compliments. Let's start again.

REBECCA   I don't think we can start again. We started . . . a long time ago. We started. We can't start *again.* We can end again.

DEVLIN   But we've never ended.

REBECCA   Oh, we have. Again and again and again. And we can end again. And again and again. And again.

DEVLIN   Aren't you misusing the word *end*? *End* means end. You can't end "again." You can only end once.

REBECCA   No. You can end once and then you can end again.

Silence.

REBECCA *(cont.) (singing softly)*   "Ashes to ashes—"

DEVLIN "And dust to dust—"

REBECCA "If the women don't get you—"

DEVLIN "The liquor must."

Pause.

DEVLIN (*cont.*) I always knew you loved me.

REBECCA Why?

DEVLIN Because we like the same tunes.

Silence.

DEVLIN (*cont.*) Listen.

Pause.

DEVLIN (*cont.*) Why have you never told me about this lover of yours before this? I have the right to be very angry indeed. Do you realize that? I have the right to be very angry indeed. Do you understand that?

Silence.

REBECCA Oh, by the way, there's something I meant to tell you. I was standing in a room at the top of a very tall building in the middle of town. The sky was full of stars. I was about to close the curtains but I stayed at the window for a time looking up at the stars. Then I looked down. I saw an old man and a little boy walking down the street. They were both dragging suitcases. The little boy's suitcase was bigger than he was. It was a very bright night. Because of the stars. The old man and the little boy were walking down the street. They were holding each other's free hand. I wondered where they were going. Anyway, I was about to close the curtains but then I suddenly saw a woman following them, carrying a baby in her arms.

Pause.

REBECCA (*cont.*)   Did I tell you the street was icy? It was icy. So she had to tread very carefully. Over the bumps. The stars were out. She followed the man and the boy until they turned the corner and were gone.

Pause.

REBECCA (*cont.*)   She stood still. She kissed her baby. The baby was a girl.

Pause.

REBECCA (*cont.*)   She kissed her.

Pause.

REBECCA (*cont.*)   She listened to the baby's heartbeat. The baby's heart was beating.

The light in the room has darkened. The lamps are very bright.

Rebecca sits very still.

REBECCA (*cont.*)   The baby was breathing.

Pause.

REBECCA (*cont.*)   I held her to me. She was breathing. Her heart was beating.

Devlin goes to her. He stands over her and looks down at her.

He clenches his fist and holds it in front of her face. He puts his left hand behind her neck and grips it. He brings her head toward his fist. His fist touches her mouth.

DEVLIN   Kiss my fist.

She does not move.

He opens his hand and places the palm of his hand on her mouth.

She does not move.

DEVLIN (*cont.*)   Speak. Say it. Say "Put your hand round my throat."

She does not speak.

DEVLIN (*cont.*)   Ask me to put my hand round your throat.

She does not speak or move.

He puts his hand on her throat. He presses gently. Her head goes back.

They are still.

She speaks. There is an echo. His grip loosens.

REBECCA   They took us to the trains

ECHO   the trains

He takes his hand from her throat.

REBECCA   They were taking the babies away

ECHO   the babies away

Pause.

REBECCA   I took my baby and wrapped it in my shawl

ECHO   my shawl

REBECCA   And I made it into a bundle

ECHO   a bundle

REBECCA   And I held it under my left arm

ECHO   my left arm

Pause.

REBECCA   And I went through with my baby

ECHO   my baby

Pause.

REBECCA   But the baby cried out

ECHO   cried out

REBECCA   And the man called me back

ECHO   called me back

REBECCA   And he said, What do you have there

ECHO   have there

REBECCA   He stretched out his hand for the bundle

ECHO   for the bundle

REBECCA   And I gave him the bundle

ECHO   the bundle

REBECCA   And that's the last time I held the bundle

ECHO   the bundle

Silence.

REBECCA   And we got on the train

ECHO   the train

REBECCA   And we arrived at this place

ECHO   this place

REBECCA   And I met a woman I knew

ECHO   I knew

REBECCA   And she said, What happened to your baby

ECHO   your baby

REBECCA   Where is your baby

ECHO   your baby

REBECCA   And I said what baby

ECHO   what baby

REBECCA   I don't have a baby

ECHO   a baby

REBECCA   I don't know of any baby

ECHO   of any baby

Pause.

REBECCA   I don't know of any baby

Long silence.

Blackout.

WEATHER FORECAST

The day will get off to a cloudy start.
It will be quite chilly
But as the day progresses
The sun will come out
And the afternoon will be dry and warm.

In the evening the moon will shine
And be quite bright.
There will be, it has to be said,
A brisk wind
But it will die out by midnight.
Nothing further will happen.

This is the last forecast.

March 2003

AFTER LUNCH

And after noon the well-dressed creatures come
To sniff among the dead
And have their lunch

And all the many well-dressed creatures pluck
The swollen avocados from the dust
And stir the minestrone with stray bones

And after lunch
They loll and lounge about
Decanting claret in convenient skulls

September 2002

MEETING

It is the dead of night

The long dead look out towards
The new dead
Walking towards them

There is a soft heartbeat
As the dead embrace
Those who are long dead
And those of the new dead
Walking towards them

They cry and they kiss
As they meet again
For the first and last time

August 2002

DEATH

Where was the dead body found?
Who found the dead body?
Was the dead body dead when found?
How was the dead body found?

Who was the dead body?

Who was the father or daughter or brother
Or uncle or sister or mother or son
Of the dead and abandoned body?

Was the body dead when abandoned?
Was the body abandoned?
By whom had it been abandoned?

Was the dead body naked or dressed for a journey?

What made you declare the dead body dead?
Did you declare the dead body dead?
How well did you know the dead body?
How did you know the dead body was dead?

Did you wash the dead body
Did you close both its eyes
Did you bury the body
Did you leave it abandoned
Did you kiss the dead body

1997